# Awakening Motion

## *A Journey*

Lester Neblett

Neblett Foundation Press

Neblett Foundation Press
P.O. Box 345
Davis, CA 95617

Book design by Lester Neblett
Cover art by Ron Henry
Cover design, interior design assistance and production by Catherine E. Campaigne
Color scanning and correction by Ron Henry

ISBN 0-9656072-0-8

Printed in Canada

Dedicated to
Avonelle Gadsby

In our desire to be separate we often forget to honor our connection to others. Our focus on discovering our true self is not exclusive of our being interconnected. This book is a reflection of twelve individuals' collective journey. The symbolism created by the words, colors, and shapes used to express their experiences will hopefully ignite the imagination of the soul and thus illuminate the eternal journey of humankind.

Eastern religious tradition holds that unity is real and the notion that we are separate entities is illusion. On the following pages "I" is the collective consciousness of:

Carin Hird

Cybel Lolley

Cynthia Adelizzi Pisani

Ellen Scher

Gina Bedrosian

Ginny Reis

Janice Silva-Moore

Julia Rubarth

Kit Jones

Lester Neblett

Michael Mesmer

Ron Henry

The color images reproduced in this book are referred to as "splats" and are expressions of those named above.

Our individual journeys contribute to a greater journey. We are part of a holographic universe, both collectively and individually. Within each of us is the entire universe. As I change I will affect the state of the hologram. Simultaneously, as the hologram changes so will I.

As you experience the images and words on the pages of this book hopefully you will be able to revisit your story, connect with the story of the group, and start to envision the unfolding story of humankind. Keeping in mind the concept that everything is interconnected may help you to welcome some of the mysteries of the universe.

As I awaken out of sleep there are many images of the night still floating and dimly mingling in my awareness with a vague sense of the coming day. Where do my dreams end and where does reality begin? Where does reality end and where do my dreams begin? Who am I?

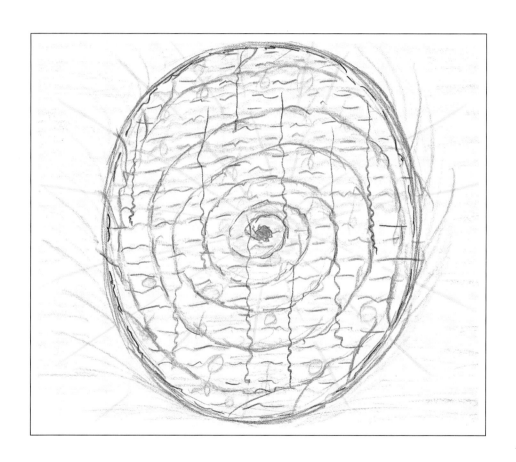

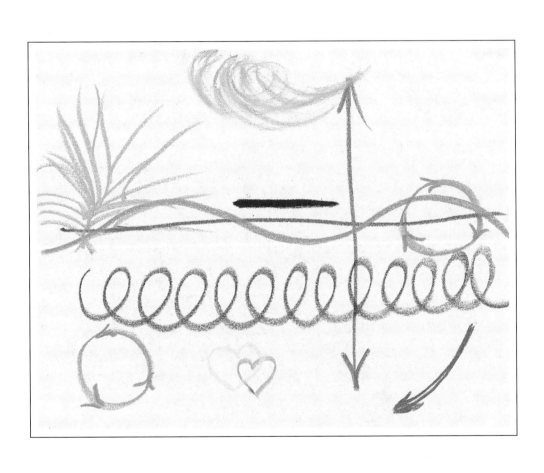

I journey with a beginner's mind.

I find myself trying to move in directions I seldom, if ever, move: inward, outward, upward, downward, backward, forward.

I feel energy flow in my body, although I am not always aware of its directions.

Wind, Water, Fire, Earth move in me and through me.

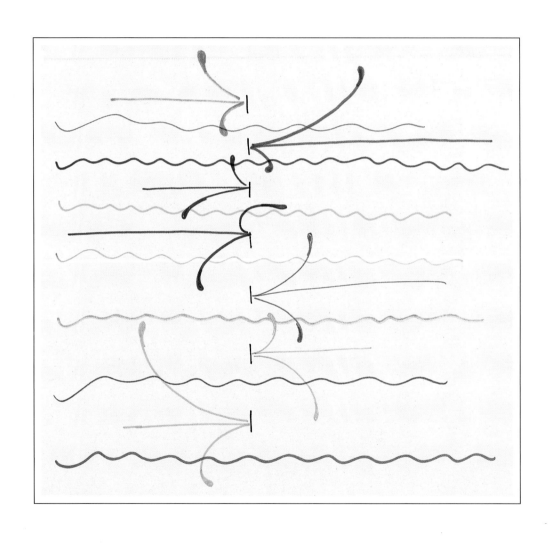

RESISTANCE, RESISTANCE, RESISTANCE. I am blocked.
How do I resist?
RESIST—*flow*RESIST—*flow*RESIST—*flow* Stop & Go
I am stuck.

    How do I get stuck?

*flow*      *flow*      *flow*      *I'm free.*      *I am open.*

    How do I *flow?*

... I feel my spine opening:
the wind,
the sinking and submersion in water
and I feel the dance of the fire.
How erratic it feels ...

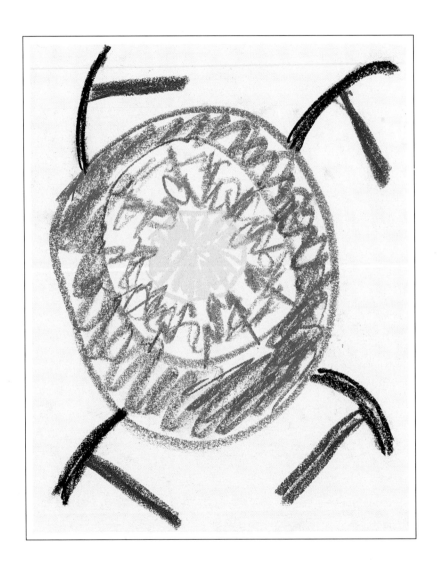

I find myself in a small, intimate group of strangers.
I am challenged to be authentic and genuine.
—to bring myself into the room—
this time my physical presence is not enough.

I Pause ...

And around the next bend my shadow is pulled into the light. I am forced to acknowledge its presence. I discover my defenses. I learn to become comfortable with being uncomfortable. And I explore Shadow's content.

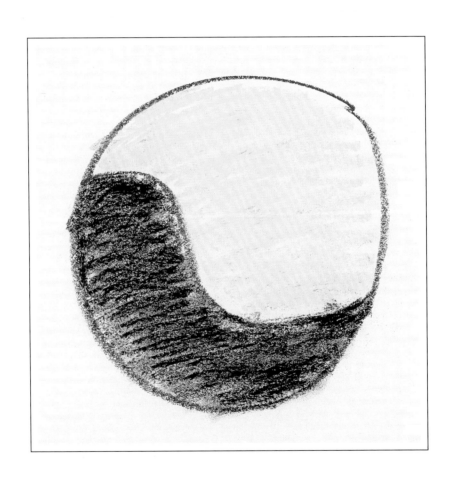

I learn to sit in silence
    To listen to my inner thoughts
        I watch my breath ...

I become aware of the rhythm of my breathing.
    As I breathe
        In and Out ...

My body relaxes, my mind quiets.

  I hug
  I embrace
  I connect
  I join . . .


                              I cry.

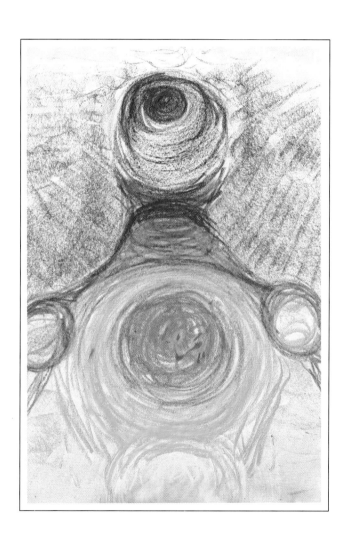

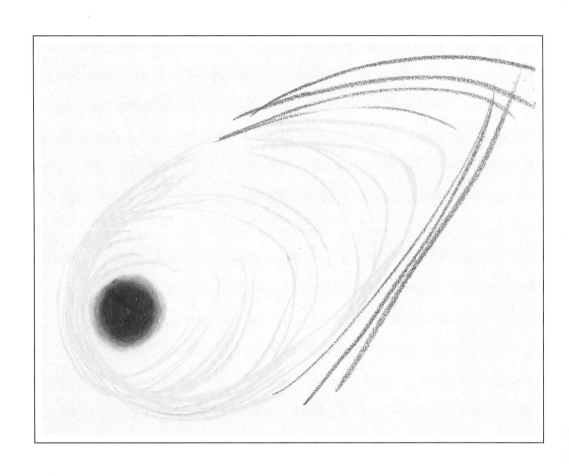

To my surprise the world has offered me another way to move. The concepts of "to be," "to be present," "to be in the moment," "to do nothing" are placed before me. I am challenged! If I am not "doing," then who am I? I am asked to be a "human being" when all I know is "human doing." "Where is 'being' to be found?" I ask.

I become reflective.

I contemplate my existence.

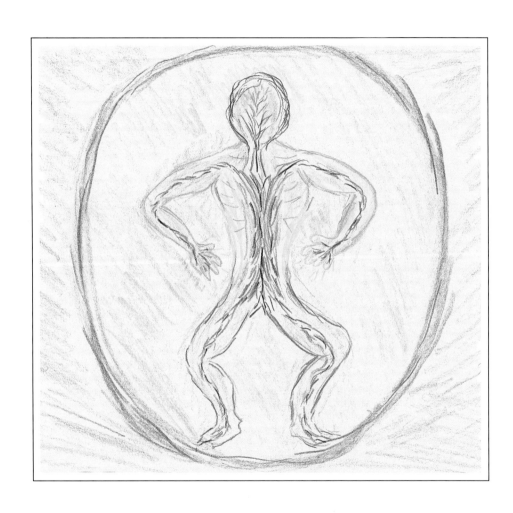

Similar to
the caterpillar I find
myself surrounded by an
invisible, nurturing cocoon;
feeling like I'm dissolving,
becoming fluid, losing my
shape. I lie in the
unknown, trusting
I am safe, wondering
what will become
of me.

I discover the edge

and feel the terror in my body. I surrender
to vulnerability as I jump into the abyss
wondering who will catch me. Will I find
my way through the darkness of the
unknown?

There are times when
I feel like the trapeze artist
Who, at a single given moment,
Has completely let go
Of the swing supporting him
And is simultaneously
Reaching for another one.
At this precise moment,
I realize there is no turning back.
I become aware
I am suspended between paradigms.

I no longer know who I am ...

I walk,
speak,
move,
breathe,

AND YET.

I am not sure who is there.
Is it me or someone else with an identical name?
And, at the same time,
I begin to question if I have ever known who I am.

At times
   I feel empty.
   I stuff my face.
   I feel confused.
   I do not sleep well.

What keeps me going?

Where am I going?

It's hard to remember now how much pain I must have been feeling to have chosen to embark on this journey. The pain I experience now is no longer denied, it moves freely, and it comes from a deeper place.

I experience my pain. I feel the loss, the hurt, the isolation, the disappointment, the abandonment, the grief, and the loneliness associated with my life. It moves through me. I feel more!

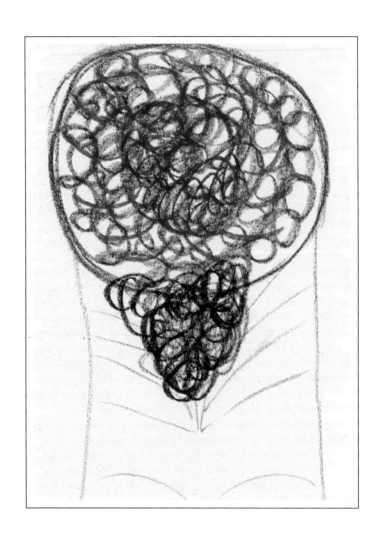

"Why me?" I ask. As I struggle to find my way, friends give me words of encouragement.

One friend offered:

"When the student is ready the teacher appears."

Another softly recited the words of Anais Nin:

"The day came for you when the risk to remain closed in a bud became more painful than the risk to blossom."

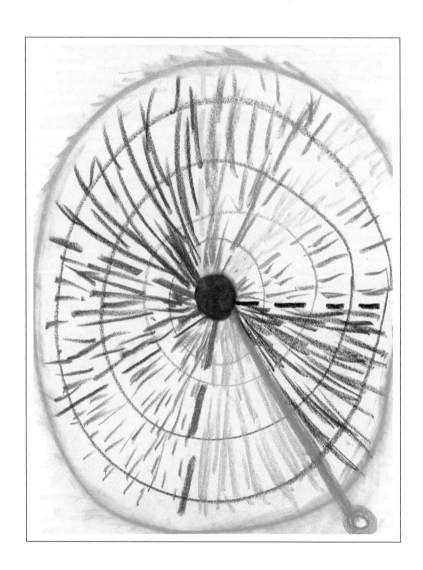

My thoughts begin to wander. I start to daydream. These words from Stuart Heller dance and play within my psyche:

As I believe, so I behave.
As I behave, so I become.
As I become, so becomes my world.

They tease me until my attention is drawn to reflect on their meaning. What do I believe? What are my beliefs? And how do they create my world? I begin to think.

Enough, Enough! I shout. This is too much!
I wish I had never started this journey.
I feel like I am spinning around and around.
I am out of control.

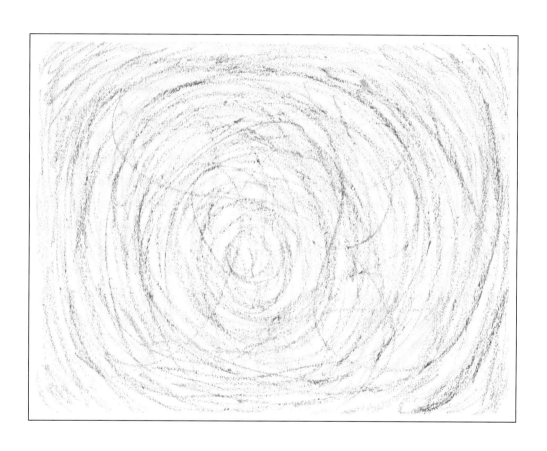

I pause to question myself . . .

I wonder if I am honoring my truth,
  if I can let go of the old so the new can come forth,
  if it is my heart or my head which is leading,
  if it is truly possible to embody heart wisdom.

And, I wonder if I can continue my journey.

I take several deeeeep, looonnnng, slooowwww, breaths . . .

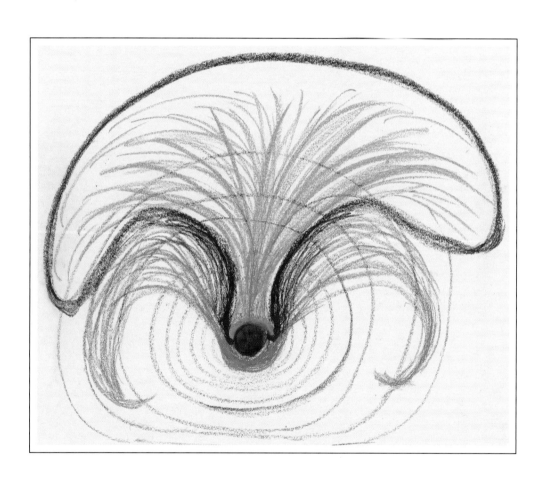

Maybe, I tell myself, this journey is just about over! At most I have a day, possibly a week and at the very most a month before my journey reaches completion! I can do anything for a month, I say to myself. I feel myself start to relax. I become aware of my breathing. I start to feel grounded. Oh, who am I kidding! I'll be in this for the rest of my life. I choose to move on.

I begin to think about the presence of angels. I wonder if everyone is blessed with an angel as their spirit guide. Sometimes I get this strange, wonderful feeling someone or something is watching over me. I feel loved and protected.

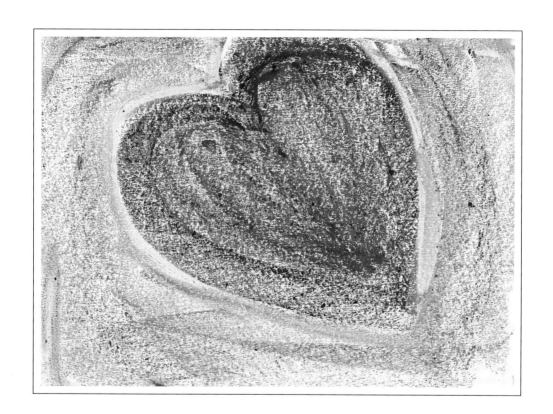

As I occasionally do, I drift from one thought to another. During this time I become aware of my noticing the people around me. I ponder their shapes. I observe differences and similarities. I wonder how many of them are ectomorphs or mesomorphs or endomorphs. I am fascinated with the preoccupation of humankind to place itself in categories. "What possible benefits come from such elaborate systems?" I ask. A wise friend offered, "It's like looking through one window to see only part of a room in a house that has many rooms and numerous windows." I pause. I think to myself, "could be, could be."

I become mindful ...

I let the silence slowly fill with the sound of music. I feel the rhythm in my gut. I feel the vibrations of the finely-tuned strings stretched from neck to belly. I hear the sounding of the next note as a key is gently touched. The sounds creatively mix, overlap, and inter-twine producing a magical moment. I am aware of the energy in my body moving freely. I feel in harmony with the universe.

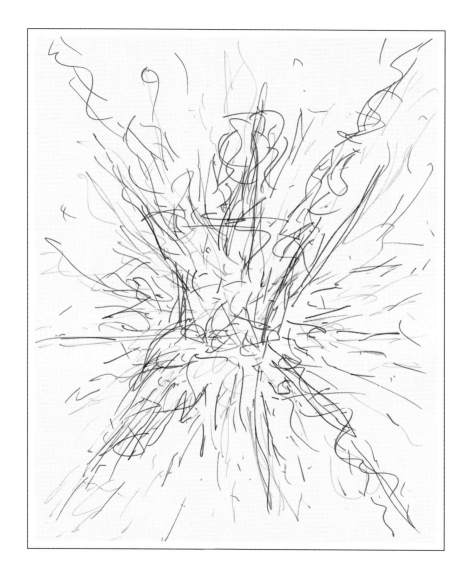

And as I continue down my path
created out of present moments,
my friends sing
this sufi song:

All I Ask Of You Is Forever To Remember Me,
As Loving You.

All I Ask Of You Is Forever To Remember Me,
As Loving You.

All I Ask Of You Is Forever To Remember Me,
As Loving You.

I watch you dissolve and re-organize
dissolve and re-organize.
And each time the new form is more
beautiful than the last.

# Acknowledgments

With each conscious breath
   I open to a deeper awareness of
   what it means to live

I find myself awe struck by the
   unexpected gifts that emerge
   from the unknown

And I'm humbled as I witness
   the unfolding of another person.

To the following people,
   I am blessed to have you in my life:

Anders Soderlund
Andy Robertson
Brett Kersten
Calvin Choy
David Hughes
Debbie Jones
Diana Hansen
Gail Olson
Karen Haas
Kathy Thompson
Kristi Robertson
Marilyn Davis
Patricia Wheeler
Peggy Rogers
Ron Luyet
Tony Cancio
Victoria Deloney
Virginia Dennehy
and My Family

# To

Ron Henry
Michael Mesmer
Kit Jones
Julia Rubarth
Janice Silva-Moore
Ginny Reis
Gina Bedrosian
Ellen Scher
Cynthia Adelizzi Pisani
Cybel Lolley
Carin Hird

We share an extraordinary journey.
Know you are a part of a very meaningful time in my life.
May you experience what brings
joy and love into your life.

A Warm Hug
Les

# About the Author

Lester Neblett received his Masters degree from John F. Kennedy University. He is the founder of the Neblett Foundation which was established in 1981. He is presently Program Director at the Cancer Support and Education Center and is an instructor for the International Training and Education Center at the University of California, Davis. His many interests include traveling, cross-cultural awareness and education, men's emotional and spiritual growth, supporting youth and adolescents, understanding and working with the mind-body-spirit connection, and the arts.

ARTISTIC TOUCH GALLERY
205 G Street, Davis, CA 95616
(916) 753-1731

CANCER SUPPORT AND EDUCATION CENTER

| Meno Park | Davis | Berkeley |
|---|---|---|
| 1035 Pine Street | 719 2nd Street | 1803 Martin Luther King |
| Menlo Park, CA 94025 | Davis, CA 95616 | Berkeley, CA 94709 |
| (415) 327-6166 | (916) 757-1251 | (510) 849-0357 |

INTERNATIONAL TRAINING AND EDUCATION CENTER
University Extension
University of California, Davis
Davis, CA 95616
(916) 757-8686

JOHN F. KENNEDY UNIVERSITY
12 Altarinda Road, Orinda, CA 94563
(510) 254-0200

NEBLETT FOUNDATION
P.O. Box 345
Davis, CA 95617